# Grace Notes

# Grace Notes
Lisa López Smith

GRAYSON BOOKS
West Hartford, Connecticut
graysonbooks.com

Grace Notes
copyright © 2021 by Lisa López Smith
published by Grayson Books
West Hartford, Connecticut
ISBN: 978-1-7364168-1-5

Interior & Cover Design by Cindy Stewart
Cover Photo: https://unsplash.com/@gpthree

*Para Luis Guillermo: Contigo, todo es menos complicado y más bonito. Te amo.
Y para Matzo & Santiago Kalil—ustedes son la razón de todo,
y Emiliano, Julia, Sofía, Andrea—son rayitos del sol en mi día.*

# Acknowledgements

"Sacred" was published in *Tiferet*, Spring 2020.

"Bullet Mushroom" was published in *Sky Island Journal*, April 2021.

"What was promised me" was published in *Coal Hill Review Literary Magazine*, November 2018.

"American Illusion" was published as "In the Templo Compañía de Jesús, Oaxaca City" with the *International Human Rights Festival*, 2019.

"Age 37" first appeared in *The Esthetic Apostle*, 2019.

"Moving the Sheep" first appeared in *The Sunlight Press*, Spring 2021.

An earlier version of 'Desconocida (Jane Doe)" appeared in *Sin Fronteras*, Issue 22, 2017.

An earlier version of 'Translating Testimony from the Ayotzinapa Investigation Report into English" was first published in *Tilde*, 2019.

"The Dirt on the Universe" was published by *Flock*, 2021.

"Sometimes" first appeared in *Sky Island Journal*, April 2019.

"Studying Arabic in Quarantine" first appeared in *K'in*, Winter 2020.


No chapbook is an island! One thousand thanks to:
Ginny Connors at Grayson Books for making this chapbook possible. So much gratitude to Cecilia Woloch, Michael Collins, Forrest Gander, Ellen Archer, Shelley Smithson, Susan Fitzky, Julianne Palumbo, Elizabeth Newdom, Maureen McVeigh, Mohamed Sorour, everyone with The Migrant Trail, y todxs con FM4 Paso Libre (Guadalajara). With thanks to Ed Smith & Jennie S. Koning for life-long cheerleading. Gracias a México, lindo y querido, mi maestro, que abre mi ojos y corazón todos los días. Luis Guillermo, estoy siempre agradecida por ti.

# Contents

| | |
|---|---|
| Sacred | 11 |
| Bullet Mushroom | 12 |
| What was promised me | 14 |
| American Illusion | 15 |
| Field Medicine | 16 |
| Age 37 | 18 |
| Return of the Butterflies | 19 |
| Moving the Sheep | 20 |
| Desconocida (Jane Doe) | 21 |
| Translating Testimony from the Ayotzinapa Investigation Report into English | 23 |
| The Dirt on the Universe (essay) | 24 |
| Sometimes | 26 |
| Studying Arabic in Quarantine | 27 |
| Sweet Little Sacraments | 29 |
| About the Author | 30 |

# Sacred

*Jalisco, Mexico*

The sun drenching the harrowed soil—will it ever produce what we desire? The sun on the crops of my neighbor, who stole the fields from his brothers and probably had a gun. Fallow. Rushing to pack the lunch bags, one of my children is missing a shoe, the six-year-old's sweater is unzipped, they wave goodbye. Finding the hawk—its body speckled like reddish sand still limp as if just asleep on the side of the road: eyes closed, grey, the talons so curved and sharp they could take off my hand. The rust on the '69 Galaxie changes color season by season, grass growing through the dashboard. The daddy long-legs cluster for warmth—a leggy, black ball of fuzz the size of my hand. Silence. My dogs collide with the front gate, with each other, with my legs, their enthusiastic frustration that my two hands can't greet all six of them at the same time. The monarch lifts and lowers her wings like the lungs of a Zen master. At the side of the road, Martín paints broad brushstrokes of sauces and oils across skewered chickens, fanning the coals volcanic red with a hairdryer; he works until he sells out every day. Padre Manuel recommended the homebrew mezcal from the third house on the left before town, just bang on the gate; we bought a bottle and everyone agreed it was bien suave. In cartel lingo, hawks are what lookouts are called  Opportunities, like food and gasoline, aren't evenly distributed, that's for sure.  Look. How the spiny paddles of nopal are transformed into narrow slices of grey-green in the salsa with onions and ruby tomatoes. Somewhere, a mother watches her sons get lookout jobs because the kids are hungry and there are bills to pay. The lamb, sleeping now beneath the turned soil; my children, who recited a Padre Nuestro for her. I tell them, look out for the good—there's probably something holy in noticing. I stop to observe the huizaches, and the cilantro in the garden, see the notebook with every page filled, the sweater with threads of dog hair stuck to it. How nothing is left. How there's nothing more to ask for.

# Bullet Mushroom

No stray bullets
of either the *fiscalía*
or the cartel

penetrated our fence line
but outside my children
find a bullet casing—

brass-colored: GFL WIN 308.
Investigating online, I discover
it's a hunting /sniper rifle casing,

barreling me into a new wiki-world: *sectional density
vs. ballistic coefficient*, and *muzzle velocity*,
and *recoil chamberings* until I understand

that this was a weapon of *high terminal performance*,
used on the highway in front of my house
by humans hunting each other on a sunny Thursday afternoon.

I go hunting for more cases along the highway, but
like watching the news, why look for more evidence for fear? Also
strange, only last month I went hunting

for mushrooms in the *cerro* and back fields:
the strangeness of foraging mushrooms the first time,
then slicing them into the pan for lunch.

They were brownish-white, firm; at least three sources confirmed their edibility, identifiable by color and shape.
The wild mushroom is a symbol of the soil reviving.

The *mycelium network* in this *agro-ecosystem* breathing
life in my backyard; the *diverse fungal populations* are essential
to *holistic farming* and *soil regeneration* and *climate mitigation*, but back to
bullets,

and people carrying them—pursued and pursuing—
how they too planted beans in plastic cups back in kindergarten,
and I wonder if their grandmothers took them foraging

for wild ciruela, nopal, hongos.
Maybe the letters stamped on a bullet casing
are all the clarification we want, simplifying

what is *good*
or *evil*. Who wouldn't
learn to kill

and pluck a chicken to feed the kids
or learn to forage if the economy evaporated again,
or how to load a gun or saddle a horse if your job required it;

we've all sat in pews listening for God,
we've watched clouds and the ribbon of highway
the wheels of unmarked vehicles passing.

# What was promised me
*after Cecilia Woloch*

Nothing. Band-Aids for broken bones. Papercuts and pebbles in my shoe. How stars feel on a clear night, trickling pixels hand over hand over sky over sea over air, to me. My grandmother's ring, never recovered. The scent of tomatoes on my fingers long afterwards, blossoms, and rootlessness. *Delfts blauw*, the wrinkled recipe card for *boterkoek* and Pake's *speculaas*—the hints of ginger and almonds like a cloak. A few whispers, a story to write, to keep. The humid scent of the night- time flowers holding me like a kiss, and a few bites of magic dust. Or beans. A fishhook and a toolbelt, rain-wrecked, shipwrecked, I wept, too. A bookshelf and a fireplace, but not at the same time, not forever. Spiderwebs with dancing rain droplets, the first snow while picking the last of the apple crop, a few constellations in a galaxy I can't see. The open road, the high seas—ship adrift, and a song.

# American Illusion

*In the Templo Compañía de Jesús, Oaxaca City*

*Don't do it,*
I want to say
with all the colonial wisdom
of my smooth border crossing,
passported, educated practicality. After all,
I once walked in the dust and sun
of the Sonoran Desert, berated
the walls, knelt at the crosses
of unknown remains,
learned just what the sun could do
to a body—rendered
unrecognizable in just one day. Before,
I had dispensed rice & beans
& slices of soap in the shelter,
there never were enough
size 28-waist pants for all
the skinny boys there.
I once translated reports
for an asylum case for a man
escaping the cartels—exit wounds,
ending bodies in acid tanks or garbage incinerators.

But what do I say?
His shirt is tucked into tidy black jeans and he carries a big duffle.
His baby daughter in her pink dress toddles by,
wearing sparkly sandals and a serious smile.

*Ah-mer-ee-can Dream*, he says,
here in this church, weeks of walking
from the border. He picks her up,
her curls bobbling.
*Ah-mer-ee-can Dream!*

We talk at the open door of the church,
between the sweaty clamor of the street outside,
and the hush of the cool interior.
All that we can't know is in the air between us.
Broken flowers
crumble between my fingers.

# Field Medicine

No stainless-steel examining table. No
air-conditioned waiting room. Holding
the IV drip up high while also keeping an eye on the ram
that charges with little warning; sun

on the back of your neck, googling symptoms
until you can finally get a vet on the line;
there are half-guess doses, figuring it out, luck, a rope, jumping
out of the way before getting kicked.

Observing: eyes, breath, ears, pace;
dirty towels, blood on the grass—as if with each step,
pulling a petal off a daisy: he loves me *hopeless*,
he loves me *hopeful*, hopeless, hopeful. Flies,

shit, a lasso, feathers and bones, finding the vein;
the hose or extension
cord never quite reaching, decoding
when to end the suffering and finding

the strength to say it out loud. Fingers stained blue
from the antiseptic, red from blood, brown
from injectable iron, or muck or mud;
there's no seatbelt on this ride, just hanging on,

making do, saying a prayer;
sweat & bad timing & patience,
and a tequila afterward by the light
of a single bulb dangling. Sitting

next to a dead horse on a hillside
under the palo dulce in the rain; working
by the light of a cell phone. Not
knowing the answers. Knowing the answers

but the *machismo* here won't fucking acknowledge it.
Too hot or too cold or too wet or too desperate.
That time with the piglet and the kitten
bundled together in a towel in a cardboard box

under the kitchen sink. Rot
and maggots; never enough, adjusting
the foot of an about-to-be born lamb, midwifed
by stars and alone, with the sky.

# Age 37

I can't say I'm discontent, mostly
things fall into their places, most things
I can accept for a time.
Until I don't. There's something
in the way maple leaves crunkle underfoot.
I once dreamed of being a shepherd,
so be careful what you wish for.
I once thought I'd give up a career track,
probably at the Embassy,
to pick grapes in France, in fact
it was apples in the Similkameen.
I thought another degree
would get me somewhere better,
but I guess I'm just thankful
I landed where I did:
on my feet, stumbling,
on my knees.
I didn't think motherhood
would suit me,
but it turns out my shape
can metamorphosize into all sorts of discomfort
and I'll like it. The truth is
I care about everything,
but am learning how to let go.
The world is too heavy most days,
but then there is a symphony on the radio,
the dandelions my children picked,
the ecstatic bawl of the lambs,
the sweet sting of the ocean's salt,
the pines' fragrance—
sharp and breathless and full of grace.

# Return of the Butterflies

I wonder if we are only one cocoon phase away
from crawling on our bellies in the dust. I wonder
if thousands of years ago the atoms of our bodies
were trees and that's what gives us the strength to hang on.
Yet every year trees shake down their leaves,
remembering to let go. I wonder
if clay feels the pain of its reformation—
or is it joy? I wonder if the dust
of our bodies decaying will turn into butterfly wings,
and really, I wonder if the return of the butterflies
each season isn't just to remind us
how far we've come,
and how little we matter.

# Moving the Sheep

there's sometimes a fear-filled lamb
taking off in the opposite direction of sense,
braying madly, as if the earth

had suddenly started spinning in reverse,
and he concludes the gate must be at the other end
of the mountain. I hike up behind him

to where the flocks scorch-earthed the grass
under the trees clustered like witches,
the clouds soft and undefined

as if a misguided watercolorist had spilled
the yellow butterflies, white ones, brown ones
flickering about the fields of October's

wildflowers, each bud waiting to burst forth,
each one in its place. Observation,
the best tool of the shepherd,

otherwise only guesses into sheep psychology.
My lamb has skittered to the back fence, and I know
his fears are as imaginary as my own.

I flush him out down below to the flock,
he gallops and hollers, angry at my interference.
No one ever said the lost sheep was grateful,

but such is the burden of the sought. The solitary
hawk above us. This tilting fence edged with barbed wire.
Quiet, and oblivious to lostness, the sheep graze on.

# Desconocida (Jane Doe)

*Sásabe, Sonora, México to Tucson, Arizona, USA*

Wooden crosses in a pile, painted white—
each bearing the name of someone
who died in the desert.

Your cross: *Desconocida*,
written in permanent marker,
the fiscal year in which
your remains were found: *2012-13*,
your age: *unknown*.

— - - — - — -

Desconocida, I imagine it is your shadow
that stretches long beside me.

This time, I walk the desert *with* you, *we* walk,
I want you to know that this time, *no estas sola*.

The morning sun hangs low.

— - - — - — -

Desconocida, this, your Via Dolorosa—
did you choose which saguaro would be your grave marker,
which olive green arms would point you towards the heavens—
an angel to hold you as you die?
Did you watch Death come creeping for you
across the indifferent Arizona sky?

— - - — - — -

Hers is not my pain to bear. But
I have decided that I will hold this discomfort close:
heat heavy,
thorn piercing my sole.

We watch the *Migra* drive by
in their dog-catcher trucks;
there are rumors of vigilantes

shooting bullets through water tanks,
an oasis, once, for sojourners in the desert, now dry.

— -- —- — -

For seven days    we walk this heat.

— -- —- — -

Desconocida,
I can almost hear your loved ones say your name.

how you tilted your head and laughed
how you coaxed the tomato blossoms
into ripe stars, how you knew
the right songs to sing to the beans in the pot
so they'd cook perfectly every time.

— -- —- — -

Walking, we the living call out the names
on each of the crosses.
Desconocida, there is a waterfall
of names echoing with yours—
the lost are still present as long
as the living say your names:

*¡Desconocida! ¡Presente!*
*¡Desconocida! ¡Presente!*

— -- —- — -

The reddish sand floats in clouds.
The *mesquite* thorn blossoms.
The sun rises until your long shadow becomes the shadow under my feet.

# Translating Testimony from the Ayotzinapa Investigation Report into English

*(Número de Investigación Preliminar)* Preliminary Investigation Number/
against
*(Quien Resulte Responsible)* Whom Is Responsible
disappearance/ kidnapping/ aggrieved/
approximately 2300 hours
forty-three students/ bus/ surveillance camera 3/ hijack//
witness with identity key "X"
also known as/
a hawk for/
Cocula landfill/remains/
and the head of assassins also known as/
also referring to/
at kilometer 154/ Highway/ without license plates
changed the numbers on the police cars/
because they were going to kill him, like they killed/
and/ and/ and/
six people with firearms/
ran away/
thorn bushes/ saw him/
"kill these people"/ under the orders of/
it was/
who first
shot/ hit him/
jawbone/
"kill them now, because it's about to rain."

# The Dirt on the Universe

The starlings, blackbirds, and turtledoves steal grain from the hens. I am the chief shit-sweeper of the hens every morning, amidst the frantic flutter of the wild birds escaping. The morning hen poop is thick and gooey, and for me shit sweeping is my daily reminder, as a rabbi advised centuries ago, to carry a paper in one pocket that says: *I am but dust and ashes*. For balance, as necessary, to pull out the paper in the other pocket: *The Universe was created for me*. I once saw the back pasture full of lightning bugs flickering in blackness, I saw the Milky Way one night in the middle of the desert. But most days have their feathers and shit.

A blind, bald starling fell out of the nest on the front patio, once, and stayed alive for four days thanks to a heating blanket and watery tuna that I tweezed into its throat with a pair of nail scissors every four hours. Then it died. As baby birds do. Why even try for four days and three long nights–as if birds could understand the language of my intentions, as if my efforts made any difference at all, as if the world needed one more starling.

The grain for the hens attracts rats so cats were a reasonable solution. One is majestic and dignified. The other is farty and drools a lot. The princess doesn't stoop to hunt, but Roy, the farty one, brought me a baby rat, leaving it decapitated in two untidy pieces on the patio. In the laundry basket, I found another baby rat, several days dead, maggots already burrowing through the dirty clothes. Roy, expectant of some appreciative token, watched me gagging in the laundry. And then, as if I weren't drowning already, another stray dog shows up. What's the difference between five dogs, and six? Or seven? Chaos is still chaos. Maybe all the disarray is compound interest on the sacred, in the same way the universe keeps expanding, the way laundry and abandoned puppies pile up.

The baby goats nibble on my hair when I crouch down to their level, perhaps because it looks like straw to them or because goats are indifferent to what anyone else believes. The more time I shepherd goats, the more I feel that they have much to teach me, sort of like the rabbi with the strips of paper in his pockets. Their language is even subtler, however. They are generous with their whole beings—giving milk and goat kids and affection, yet they also march around this kingdom with those horns like middle fingers directed at the world; fences and rules be damned. *We can be both*, I think is what they'd say if we spoke the same language. But, who listens to goats?

The whole planet is seven billion threads both knotting together and simultaneously tearing apart. I knot myself closer when I can because humans are not meant to be islands. I learned to speak Portuguese by memorizing Bandeira's poem, "Canção do vento e da minha vida" *(Song of the wind and of my life)*. When I try to speak Italian, now it comes out in Spanish. I don't go to church, but I have walked across the Sonoran Desert. I'm the child of immigrants and am an emigrant; these are some of my own tiny knots, loosening and tightening. When my Mexican neighbors talk about crossing to the States, fear runs through my body, cold like the desert night. We all want the same thing for our children. I preen and fuss and tuck the blankets around my own boys at night like a hen arranging the eggs under the safe warmth of her feathers. We all do.

The stars don't move as I float in the water, nothing between me and infinity but gases and galaxies. Bandeira wrote,
*O vento varria as luzes, (the wind sweeps the lights)*
*O vento varria as músicas, (the wind sweeps the songs)*
*O vento varria os aromas, (the wind sweeps the scents)*
*And my life became evermore*
*Full of scents, of stars, of songs.*

I hold my breath underwater looking at the sky and thinking that the world has a long way to go, and sometimes the mess overwhelms me. It's like this translation I was working on: I had to research functions of automatic weapons: magazines, cartridges, shells, to find the right English words. I had to research the alphabet soup of kidnapping departments and police jargon. I was doing a translation about forty-three students who got disappeared one night in Guerrero. Forty-three names, forty-three poems, forty-three teenagers training to be teachers.

One of the speckled hens rolls in her dust bath, tossing reddish powdery earth over herself. So it goes: one language turning into another, goat milk into cheese, life into death, and also, cleaning the same chicken shit every day. But when I angle my view just right—holding breath in my lungs until it hurts and I lift my own wobbly song—it is an offering, of dirt and snot and flowers.

# Sometimes

Sometimes the day is enough just as it is.
Sometimes you'll actually notice it—the clouds frothy angel wings
or a frosty layer of ice across the windshield of the sky,
the snowy *garza* practically floating across the treetops,
the way the sun angles down through the tall grass,
and that day could have sailed by just like a thousand others,
except this time,
you saw it.
Sometimes the right song comes on the radio.
You're still sitting there long after the final chords fade
into chittering about the weather,
because something in that strain was the mix
of how your day's been going now that you've read the news
about Syria and Yemen,
and the prostitutes in New York, and
how your children bundled their first fallen teeth
into a ream of toilet paper stuffed under their pillow.
Sometimes we'll remember there's enough to share—
make that table stretch to the far side of the earth and really,
the abundance should surprise no one who's harvested tomatoes
and zucchini in late summer, the heat rising from the soil,
the leaves prickling your fingers,
the scent of sunshine and basil,
the grit under your nails.
Sometimes you'll remember how it feels to be alone—
those times your tears soaked through all the pillowcases,
and even the cat walked off.
You'll scrape your crumpled ménage of blood, bones, and water off the floor,
and bravely masked,
you'll remember to say something extra nice to the cashier
or you'll leave a bill instead of the coins for the guy waiting your table, and
you'll let the dog snuffle into your ear
until at last,
you smile.
Sometimes a day is enough to leave you in pieces.
Sometimes the night will put you back together. Or not.
Sometimes the earth under your body is all you need,
grass and life thrumming up to touch
all the places it hurts,
and the stars blinking like a heartbeat.

# Studying Arabic in Quarantine
*Jalisco, Mexico*

1.
With my morning *qahua* (قهوة)
steaming in its cup, and an app,
I try teaching myself Arabic
(as if one day we might travel again)
as always, interrupted by kids, the goats
trapezing across fence lines again,
another stray dog—or five,
by Spanish confounding Portuguese,
and listening to a new podcast in Italian
while painting the kitchen tangy green.

2.
Translate to English:
ما هذا؟
What is this?

(Maybe it's time to see things differently?)
Meanwhile, each sound fumbles on my lips,
tongue twisting shapes,
and drawing curves, swoops, dashes
as if I'm in kindergarten.

Translate to English:
أين أنا؟
Where am I?

(my pages start reflecting
my life
back to front)
everything illegible,
the struggle to parse meaning
from unfamiliar shapes & forces.

3.
Yet I and this phoenix world
continually rebirthing—
our awkward lips learning to speak something
completely new—

الحمد لله
Praise be to God.

4.
Translate to Arabic:
The kids pass the afternoon picking guamúchiles
under the desert-hot sun.

Translate to Arabic:
Hear the songs from mourning doves,
smell the pomegranate fresh off the tree,
watch the ribbon of goats
trickle down the barren hillside toward home

meanwhile my phone pings reminders:
trace vowel composites,
grapple throaty growls,
meanwhile the kids cut up mangoes for dinner,
meanwhile we go nowhere
but make this road by walking it.

5.
All those unwieldly days,
cloistered at home,
still
أنا لا أعرف
I don't know.

Yet sheltered in words
and in every single language
they tell me
I've always been home.

# Sweet Little Sacraments

A blade of grass on the tongue,
these grace notes
of summer night bonfires,
two pajama-clad princes in rubber boots
dancing bare-chested
stabbing marshmallows into the ashes,
the back fields,
fireflies,
distant lightning,
swallows on the wire,
frog song from the bog,

the spirit
blowing through
like a force field.

# About the Author

Originally from the west coast of Canada, Lisa López Smith has lived and worked in Italy, Uganda, China, the USA, and Brazil, but Mexico has her heart. Along with her *tapatío* husband and sons, she raises livestock on their biodynamic farm. She has a BA from the University of Calgary and an MA from Royal Roads University in subjects unrelated to writing or farming, and her poems and essays have been nominated for Best of the Net and the Pushcart Prize. *Grace Notes* is her first chapbook, selected by Cortney Davis as the winner in Grayson Books' annual chapbook prize contest. She has volunteered with FM4 Paso Libre, a migrant center in Guadalajara and walked across the Sonoran Desert with The Migrant Trail to remember the lives lost in crossing. When not wrangling kids or rescue dogs or goats, you can probably find her wandering the wild spaces of Jalisco on bike or horseback.

www.ingramcontent.com/pod-product-compliance
Lightning Source LLC
Chambersburg PA
CBHW062208100526
44589CB00014B/2006

# Winner
## 2021 Grayson Books Chapbook Competition

I'm just knocked out by the beauty of these poems, poem after poem, as they swerve from aching joy to restless gratitude to quietly heart-broken horror to hope and all the way back again. They grapple with terror and violence and the abundant earth and a mother's love, and each one soars, lifting off the page, lifting me.
—Cecilia Woloch, author of *Sur la Route*

Praise be the poet who can see the sacred in the Milky Way as much as in "the sweater with threads of dog hair." I love the exquisite wisdom of these prayers to the every-day. "I don't go to church," the poet admits, "but I have walked across the Sonoran Desert." For me, that's all the gospel I need.
—Sandra Cisneros, author of *The House on Mango Street*

This poet has things to teach us. She is a reliable guide to a harrowing world of border crossings and risk, the touchstones of earth and stars, the grittiness of field medicine and farming, and the sweet reprieve of children dancing at the close of day. This chapbook indeed offers us poems of grace, but this is a necessary grace that shakes us up: "the spirit / blowing through / like a force field."
—Cortney Davis, author of *I Hear Their Voices Singing*

Full of daily miracles, suffused with the sense that we share this astonishing planet with one another, no matter how near or far flung, no matter what language we speak…these poems are powerful, timely testimonials on how grace arises as "wobbly song—an offering, of dirt and snot and flowers."
—Ravi Shankar, author of *Correctional*

The spirit of vigilance and of loving attention suffuses these richly detailed poems of the Sonoran Desert…Lisa López Smith's poems are blessedly sane, empathetic, and wide-awake; she has a gift for transforming the gritty everyday into something hopeful, captivating, and sacramental."
—Cyrus Cassells, author of *The Gospel According to Wild Indigo*

My only criticism of this fine chapbook is that it isn't longer. A treat from the great state of Jalisco.
—Luis Alberto Urrea, author of *The Devil's Highway*

GraysonBooks.com

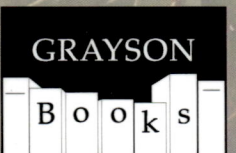

$12.00
ISBN 978-1-7364168-1-5

Book & Cover Design: Cindy Stewart

# I Am Enough

## Self-Reflection and Motivation for Women and Young Ladies

### Dr. Shanelle Fields, LPC